More Monster JOKES

A Buddy Book
by **Ima Laffin**

Buddy BOOKS

More Jokes!

VISIT US AT

www.abdopub.com

Published by ABDO Publishing Company, 4940 Viking Drive, Suite 622, Edina, Minnesota 55435.
Copyright © 2005 by Abdo Consulting Group, Inc. International copyrights reserved in all countries. No
part of this book may be reproduced in any form without written permission from the publisher.

Printed in the United States.

Edited by: Sarah Tieck
Contributing Editors: Jeff Lorge, Michael P. Goecke
Graphic Design: Deborah Coldiron
Illustrations by: Deborah Coldiron and Maria Hosley

Library of Congress Cataloging-in-Publication Data

Laffin, Ima, 1970-
   More monster jokes / Ima Laffin.
      p. cm. — (More jokes!)
   Includes index.
   ISBN 1-59197-874-2
      1. Monsters—Juvenile humor. 2. Riddles, Juvenile. I. Title. II. Series.

PN6231.M665L35 2005
818'.5402—dc22

                                        2004057516

How do monsters count to 13?
On their fingers!
How do they count to 47?

They take off their socks and count their toes!

What do you call a huge, ugly, slobbering, furry monster with cotton balls in his ears?

Anything you like. He can't hear you!

Green hairy monster: I was in the zoo last week.

Yellow bumpy monster: Really? Which cage were you in?

What's big, green, and sits in the corner all day?

The incredible sulk!

What happened when two huge monsters ran in a race?

One ran in short bursts, the other ran in burst shorts!

What should you do if a monster runs through your front door?

Run through the back door!

What kind of monster has the best hearing?

The ear-iest one!

What did the angry monster do when he got his gas bill?

He exploded!

Why are most monsters covered in wrinkles?

Have you ever tried to iron a monster?

John: I can lift a monster with one hand.
Bobby: Bet you can't!

John: Find me a monster with one hand and I'll prove it!

What's big and ugly and bounces?

A monster on a pogo stick!

What did the monster say when he fell in love with a grand piano?

"Darling, you've got lovely teeth!"

What happened to the monster
who ran away with the circus?

The police made him bring it back!

Can a monster jump higher than a
lamppost?

Yes. Lampposts can't jump!

What's big and ugly and goes up
and down?

A monster in an elevator!

What do you get if you cross a
man-eating monster with a skunk?

A very ugly smell!

How do you know that there's a monster in your bath?

You can't get the shower curtain closed!

Jenny: I'm going to keep this monster under my bed.
Beth: But what about the smell?
Jenny: He'll just have to get used to it!

Why couldn't the swamp creature go to the party?

Because he was bogged down by homework!

What happened when the monster fell down a well?

He kicked the bucket!

Did you hear about the stupid monster who hurt himself while he was raking up leaves?

He fell out of a tree!

What do young female monsters do at parties?

They go around looking for edible bachelors!

A little monster was learning to play the violin. He asked his big brother how he sounded. "You should be on the radio," his brother told him. "You think I'm that good?" he asked excitedly. "No," his brother said.

"But if you were on the radio, I could turn you off!"

Jane: Dad, what has a purple body with yellow spots, eight hairy legs, and big slimy eyes?
Dad: I don't know. Why?

Jane: Because one just crawled up your pants leg!

14

Why did Frankenstein's monster give up boxing?

Because he didn't want to spoil his looks!

Slimy monster: My brother is at medical school.
Furry monster: What's he studying?
Slimy monster: Nothing! They're studying him!

What happened when the big, dirty monster became a chimney sweep?
He started a grime wave!

When do banshees howl?
On moan-day night!

Did the bionic monster have a brother?
No, but he had lots of tran-sisters!

What happened when the scary monster stole a pig?

The pig squealed to the police!

What does a monster do when he loses a hand?

He goes to a secondhand shop!

Purple monster: Did you ever see anyone like me before?

Katie: Yes, once. But I had to pay admission!

Mrs. Monster: Will you love me when I'm old and ugly?

Mr. Monster: Darling, of course I do!

18

How can you tell if there's a
monster under your bed?

When your face is nearly touching
the ceiling!

Green monster: I've just changed my mind!

Blue monster: Does it work any better?

Monster: I'm so ugly.
Ghost: It's not that bad!
Monster: It is! When my father was born they threw a party. When I was born they threw up!

What is the best way to speak to a monster?
From a long distance!

What do you give a scuba-diving monster with big feet?
Big flippers!

Blue monster: I have a hunch.
Green monster: I thought you were a funny shape.

21

How do you tell a good monster from a bad one?

If it's a good one you will be alive to talk about it later!

Did you hear about the monster who had an extra pair of hands?

He kept them in a handbag!

What time is it when a monster sits on your car?

Time to get a new car!

What do you get if you cross a monster's brain with a rubber band?

A real stretch of the imagination!

What do you call a mouse that can pick up a monster?

Web Sites